THE STORY OF THE EARTH
VOLCANO

LIONEL BENDER

FRANKLIN WATTS
London · New York · Toronto · Sydney

© 1988 Franklin Watts

First published in Great Britain by
Franklin Watts
12a Golden Square
London W1

First published in the USA by
Franklin Watts Inc.
387 Park Avenue South
New York. N.Y. 10016

First published in Australia by
Franklin Watts Australia
14 Mars Road
Lane Cove
NSW 2066

UK ISBN: 0 86313 704 0
US ISBN: 0 531 10553 9
Library of Congress Catalog Card
No: 87 51706

Printed in Belgium

Consultant Dougal Dixon

Designed by Ben White

Picture research by Jan Croot

Produced by Lionheart Books
10 Chelmsford Square
London NW10 3AR

Illustrations:
Peter Bull Art

Photographs
J. Allan Cash Ltd 16
GeoScience Features *cover*, 9, 11, 27, 28
Hutchinson Library 17, 19, 29
Rex Features/Sipa Press 1, 13, 14, 15
Survival Anglia 7, 21, 23, 24, 25
ZEFA 10, 12, 22, 31

THE STORY OF THE EARTH
VOLCANO

LIONEL BENDER

CONTENTS

Introduction

This book tells the story of a typical volcano. It explains how the volcano is formed and what happens when it erupts. It also looks at the different kinds of volcanoes in the world. Some are active, constantly belching out smoke and red-hot liquid rock. Others are just sleeping, showing little or no sign of their violent past.

▽ A volcano usually forms when hot molten, or liquid, rock from inside the Earth is forced up through the surface. As the molten rock spews out of the top of the volcano it flows downward over the surrounding land. Slowly it cools and hardens into solid rock. Each time the volcano erupts, more molten material is forced out until layer upon layer of rock is formed.

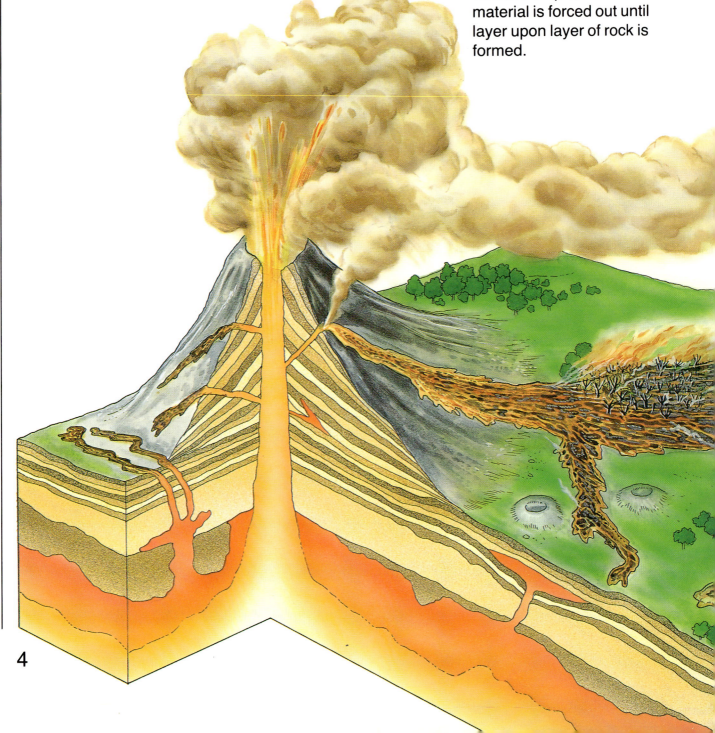

We have divided our story of a volcano into ten stages, as shown in the small pictures below. At first the volcano is calm and quiet. Then suddenly it erupts, throwing out a mixture of gases and rocks, as shown in the main illustration below. Finally, the volcano becomes quiet, but it may erupt again.

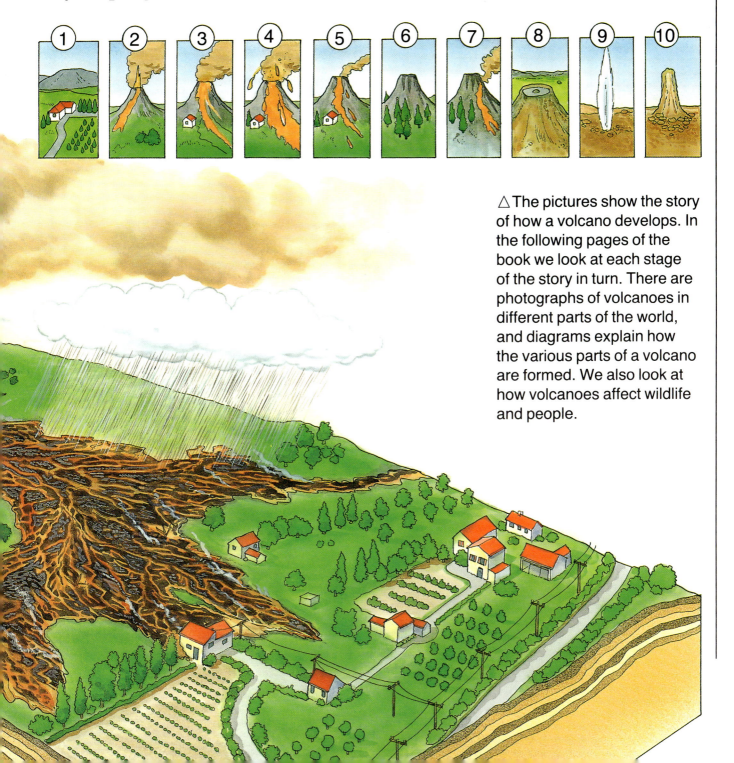

△ The pictures show the story of how a volcano develops. In the following pages of the book we look at each stage of the story in turn. There are photographs of volcanoes in different parts of the world, and diagrams explain how the various parts of a volcano are formed. We also look at how volcanoes affect wildlife and people.

There are usually clear signs that the volcano is about to erupt. First, the ground starts to shake. Then, as hot molten rock gathers under the surface, the sides of the cone bulge out. Gases pour out of cracks in the rock. Foul-smelling sulfur fumes trapped in the molten rock escape as the rock reaches the Earth's surface. But these signals do not tell us exactly when the volcano will erupt. There may be no warning at all.

▷A volcano usually looks like a cone-shaped mountain with a hole in the top. This volcano is on White Island, New Zealand. The hole is called a vent, and the molten material comes up through it. The vent becomes wider at the top and forms a hollow, or crater.

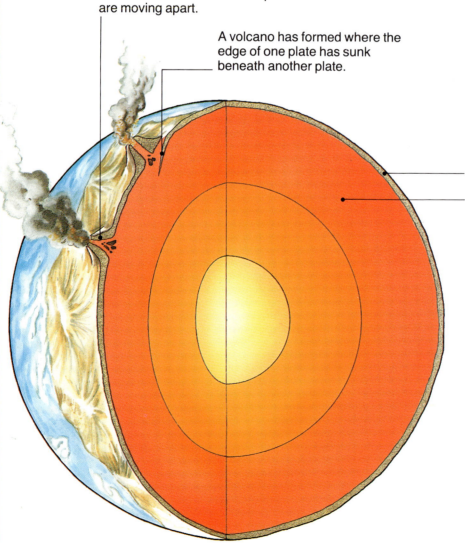

A volcano has formed where plates are moving apart.

A volcano has formed where the edge of one plate has sunk beneath another plate.

Crust

Mantle

◁The outer surface of the Earth is called the crust. It is made up of platelike slabs of solid rock hundreds of miles across. These plates float on a layer of hot liquid rock called the mantle. Where plates meet and rub together, the edge of one plate sometimes slides under the one next to it. Volcanoes often form at these places. Volcanoes also form where plates are moving apart.

When the volcano erupts, red-hot molten material bursts out. The ground shakes and trembles. Gases, dust, steam and all kinds of hot rock are blasted out of the vent high into the air. The noise of the eruption is deafening and frightening. Sometimes a volcano is blown apart completely in just a few minutes. People have no time to escape. All living things may be killed by the poisonous gases and chunks of rock thrown out by the blast.

▽ Where one plate of the crust slides beneath another, cone-shaped volcanoes form. Here the molten rock is thick and sticky like glue. It quickly cools and hardens into a gray-colored rock. These volcanoes erupt very violently. They usually occur in mountainous areas.

▷ Molten rock and gases gush out of the vent of a volcano in Hawaii in the Pacific Ocean. Volcanoes like this form where the crust is splitting apart. They are usually broad and flat. That is because the molten rock is very runny. It flows a long way before it cools and hardens into solid black rock. Most of these volcanoes form on the sea bed.

A cone-shaped volcano with a single vent.

A broad, flat volcano with several vents.

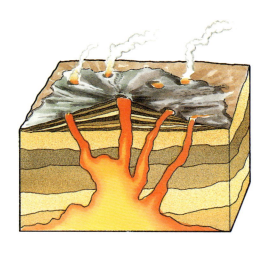

After the giant blast of the eruption, magma spews out. This is the red-hot liquid rock from the Earth's mantle deep underground. When magma reaches the surface, it gives off gases and steam. The magma is then known as lava. The force of the eruption may squirt lava into the air, creating "fire fountains" and glowing rivers of molten rock. The lava flow flattens trees and buildings in its path. Whole villages and forests may be destroyed.

▷Fiery-red lava flowing from the volcano of Kilauea, Hawaii, lights up the night sky. The Hawaiian islands poke out of the sea directly over a part of the Earth's surface where new crust is forming. There are many active volcanoes here, with lava spilling out and spreading over the land. Where the lava flows into the sea, steam billows up from beneath the waves.

◁As lava creeps down the sides of Mount Etna, in Sicily, local villagers look on in despair. The volcano is always a threat to their homes and farmland. The lava is stiff and slow-moving, but the people are powerless to keep it from flowing. The lava brings with it huge chunks of solidified rock.

Ash and bombs

The hot magma cools as it rises to the surface. Some of it becomes solid on the way up. The solid pieces are blasted out in the eruption. The smallest pieces – about the size of marbles – are known as ash, and the larger ones as bombs. Some volcanoes do not produce any liquid lava – just ash and bombs. In AD 79 the volcano Vesuvius in Italy erupted in this way, completely burying the nearby town of Pompeii.

▽ An oval bomb from a volcano in Java, Southeast Asia. The outside of the bomb cracked as it cooled, like the crust on a loaf of bread. Sometimes a lump of molten lava thrown into the air cools into a solid bomb as it flies. These bombs are often shaped like a teardrop and can be as large as a car.

◁ The volcano on the Icelandic island of Heimaey erupted in 1973. All the people on the island had to be taken off. A long river of lava threatened to block the harbor, and the town of Vestmannaeyjar was buried deep in a layer of ash. The eruption lasted many days.

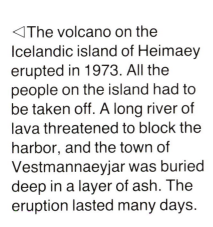

As well as lava and ash, the volcano belches out steam and gases. The steam comes from water that has seeped through the rocks from the sea or from rivers. The water boils when it reaches the magma. Once the steam is blown into the air, it cools and forms water droplets. There may be so much steam that it makes a great rainstorm. When the rain mixes with the ash that has just fallen, it forms a thick black mud.

▽ A flow of volcanic mud swept through the town of Armero in Colombia, South America, in 1986, killing many people. The water that produced the mud probably came from a nearby mountain glacier – a river of ice formed from heavy snows. The glacier was melted by the heat of the volcano.

The mud may gush downhill, washing away houses and causing as much damage as the lava. Gases given off by the magma include poisonous sulfur fumes and carbon dioxide. If produced in great quantities, such gases may choke people and wildlife in the area.

△ In 1986, in Cameroon, West Africa, many farmers and their animals died when carbon dioxide gas belched out from Lake Nios, a lake in the crater of a volcano. The gas had been collecting in the lake for some time, then suddenly fizzed out like the gas from a bottle of soda.

After a few days or perhaps months the eruption stops and the volcano goes quiet – it becomes dormant. The vent becomes blocked and the crater fills with rock material. Snow that falls on the summit is no longer melted by the heat. Glaciers may form in cold valleys. The volcano becomes just another mountain. It may stay like that for years or forever. But there is always the chance that it will burst into life again.

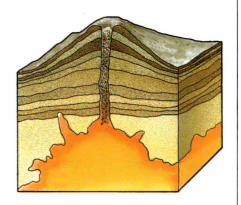

△ A volcano usually becomes dormant when the vent is blocked by hardened lava. This mass of solid rock is called a plug. Deep down, however, the magma may still be molten.

◁ Mount St. Helens in Washington State, erupted violently in 1980. A few months later the eruption stopped, but not before it had destroyed the forest for miles around.

▷ In this photo, taken five years later, plants are growing on the mountainsides and animals have moved back into the area.

Life returns

Wildlife is quick to return to an area badly damaged by a natural disaster. A volcano may erupt and destroy an island or a whole area of countryside. However, soon after the volcano becomes dormant, plants start to grow on the lava slopes. On volcanic islands, plants grow from seeds that are blown there on the wind. Insects and birds fly to the islands. Finally people sail to the islands and settle, building villages and farms on the rich soil.

▷Mosses are usually the first plants to start growing again on a volcanic island. They grow in cracks between the bare rocks and soon form soil in which larger plants can grow.

Insects such as beetles and butterflies are the first animals to arrive, attracted by the flowers. They in turn attract passing birds. Large animals such as snakes and goats may reach the islands on trees washed away from the mainland by floods.

▷ The dark soil that forms from volcanic ash is full of the chemicals plants need to grow. Many farmers are willing to risk working in a volcanic area, such as here on the island of Java, because of the fine crops that can be produced.

You cannot trust a volcano. A volcano may be dormant for hundreds of years, perhaps for so long that people have forgotten that it was a volcano. Then suddenly and with very little warning the volcano erupts once more. The eruption is likely to be very powerful and fierce. The plug of the dormant volcano prevents the magma from rising. Eventually the pressure beneath the plug builds up so much that the mass of solid rock cannot hold the magma back. The plug gives way in a huge explosion and the mountainside is ripped apart.

▷ In 1883, an old but active volcano on the island of Krakatoa in Indonesia erupted once more. First there were a few small explosions. Then the volcano blew apart with the loudest bang ever recorded. Ash blasted upward to a height of more than 80 km (50 miles) and huge sea waves swept the coasts of the East Indies. Today the remains of the volcano are still active.

◁ When a dormant volcano becomes active again, it does not always erupt from the original vent. The first vent may be blocked so tightly that the magma forces a new vent at the side of the cone. Hot ash and gas then burst through this hole.

The volcano may die down just as quickly and surprisingly as it started. The magma below may sink back into the depths of the Earth. Rock supporting the volcano may weaken so that the cone collapses inward. If the center of the volcano sinks, a huge round crater forms. This is called a caldera. Often the caldera fills with water, creating a circular lake. Further eruptions may produce tiny volcanoes on the floor of the caldera beneath the water.

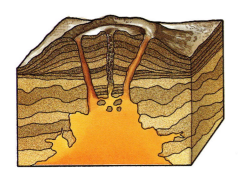

△ Magma falling away beneath a volcano can produce a wide caldera that is hundreds of feet deep. The sides of the caldera are usually steeply sloped.

◁ Crater Lake in Oregon, is a caldera that formed about 6,000 years ago. Since then the volcano has erupted and produced a new cone that sticks up in the middle of the lake.

△ The calderas of Blue Lake and Emerald lake in Tongariro National Park, New Zealand. As well as these dormant volcanoes, there are still some active ones on the island.

23

After a volcano has become dormant, there may still be evidence of the heat that once existed in the area. The rocks deep down may still be hot. Rainwater seeping down through these rocks is heated up. It then bubbles to the surface in springs and fountains of steaming hot water. In areas such as Yellowstone Park in the Rocky Mountains, there have been no volcanoes for millions of years, but the land is dotted with hot springs.

▷A geyser is a fountain of hot water. It forms when water is boiled underground by hot rocks. Bubbles of steam push up the water until it is forced out at the surface of the Earth. The fountain rises and falls because once the steam has all escaped, it takes time for the pressure to build up again.

◁Sometimes the hot water mixes with the soil and chemicals underground and produces hot mud pools. These boil and bubble at the surface of the Earth. Many different kinds of chemicals are brought to the surface, creating mud pools of different colors.

Eventually all the volcanic activity in an area dies out completely. The geysers and mud pools fizzle out and the caldera fills in. The volcano becomes a silent mountain and, like all mountains, steadily crumbles away. Over thousands of years it will be worn down to a stump and finally to totally flat land. The vents and channels that once carried the liquid magma to the surface may remain visible at the surface longer than the cone, but in time these too are turned to dust.

▷ In Tequila, Mexico, the plug of a volcano stands high above the surrounding countryside. The sides of the cone have been worn away. Their rock material helped to create the rich soil in which plants now thrive around the plug.

▷ The last sign that there was ever a volcano in an area is a tower of rock. This was once the plug of solid magma that blocked the vent of the volcano. The rock is harder than that of the sides of the cone and so is worn away more slowly by the wind and rain.

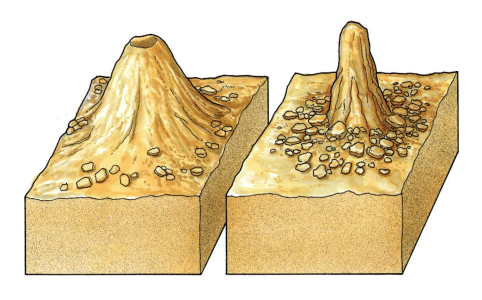

At some time in the past, there has been a volcano in almost every part of the world. Today, many people live alongside active volcanoes. Sometimes volcanoes can be useful. In Iceland, New Zealand and Hawaii the steam and hot water they create are used for heating houses and for generating electricity. Volcanic soil is very rich in chemicals needed by plants, so it is good for growing crops.

▽ A power station in New Zealand uses the steam from a volcano to produce electricity. This source of natural power is likely to last for thousands of years.

△ In Bali, Indonesia, rice is grown in the mineral-rich volcanic soil. The hills are so steep that the farmers have cut steps, or terraces, on their slopes to prevent the valuable soil from being washed away in the rains.

29

Glossary

Ash Small pieces of lava blown out of a volcano during an eruption.

Bomb A large lump of lava thrown out of a volcano during an eruption. A bomb usually starts as a flying blob of lava but solidifies as it falls to the ground.

Caldera A large circular hollow, usually over a mile in diameter, produced when a volcano collapses in upon itself.

Crater The opening at the top of a volcano produced by the explosion of an eruption. It is smaller than a caldera.

Crust The outer layer, or skin, of the Earth. The crust is about 40 km (25 miles) thick below the continents and 10 km (about 6 miles) thick below the oceans.

Dormant Sleeping. A dormant volcano is one that has not erupted for some time but may erupt again in the future. Compare with *Extinct*.

Eruption The outburst of lava, ash and gas from a volcano.

Extinct Dead. An extinct volcano will never erupt again.

Fire fountain A continuous spray of red-hot molten lava from the crater of a volcano. It is usually produced during an eruption of a broad, flat volcano rather than a cone-shaped volcano.

Geologist A scientist who studies the structure, formation and natural processes of the Earth.

Geyser A fountain of hot water and steam, spouting from the ground every few minutes in a volcanic area. It occurs when water in the ground comes in contact with hot rock.

Lava The molten rock that is thrown out of the Earth during a volcanic eruption. It is magma that has lost all its gases but is still liquid. There are two main types: thick, sticky lava, and liquid runny lava.

Magma The molten rock below the Earth's surface. At the surface, magma produces lava, ash and volcanic gases.

Mantle The layer of molten or red-hot liquid rock deep beneath the surface of the Earth.

Plate A section of the surface or crust of the Earth which floats on the mantle layer. The crust consists of about six major plates. Each plate is growing along one edge and being destroyed along another. Volcanoes form along these edges.

Plug A tower of solid lava that blocks the vent of a volcano. The plug, being made of very hard rock, is the last part of a volcano to be worn away by wind and rain.

Rock Any hard substance that is formed by the natural processes of the Earth. Some rocks are formed when lava from a volcano solidifies. Other, softer rocks are formed from layers of mud, sand and dead creatures that settle in lake bottoms or on the sea bed.

Vent A hole at the top or on the side of a volcano through which magma rises to the surface during an eruption.

Facts about volcanoes

The tallest volcano
The tallest volcano known is on the planet Mars. Olympus Mons, an extinct volcano, rises 29 km (18 miles) above the base and is 600 km (370 miles) in diameter.

Compared with that, Volcan Antofalla in Argentina, the world's highest active volcano, stands only 6.1 km (20,015 ft) tall. Cerro Aconcagua, also in Argentina, is the highest extinct volcano on Earth. It is 6.9 km (22,835 ft) high.

The most violent eruption
The eruption of Tambora in Indonesia in 1815 left a caldera 6 km (4 miles) across.

The largest caldera
The largest on Earth is Lake Toba in Sumatra. It measures 50 km (31 miles) long and 20 km (12½ miles) wide. The caldera of Olympus Mons on Mars is 70 km (44 miles) across.

The newest volcano
In 1963 a brand new volcano appeared in the ocean 32 km (20 miles) southwest of Iceland. After two years it had formed an island 2.5 km (1½ miles) in diameter. The island was called Surtsey.

The loudest explosion
The eruption of Krakatoa in Indonesia in 1883 produced an explosion that could be heard in Australia, 4,000 km (2,500 miles) away.

The greatest loss of life
Between 30,000 and 40,000 people died in the town of St. Pierre in Martinique in the West Indies when Mont Pelée erupted in 1902.

▷A village church stands on the side of a volcano on the Greek island of Santorini. In about 1500 BC the island was blown apart by an eruption as violent as that of Tambora. The volcano is now dormant.

31

Index

PRINTED IN BELGIUM BY
proost
INTERNATIONAL BOOK PRODUCTION